What is the difference between Linguistic Imperialism and Language Imperialism?

Imperialism, according to the *Merriam Webster Dictionary*, is "the extension or imposition of power, authority, or influence" over another nation. Consequently, linguistic imperialism is the extension or imposition of one's own language over another's. Martin Luther's *Bible* translation is a good example, Georg Hegel's German *Die Philosophie der Weltgeschichte* (1830) is another; the former made the *Bible* German, the latter made world history German. Language imperialism is more surgical than that: It is the translation of foreign key terminologies into familiar vocabulary of one's own language tradition in order to claim *deutungshoheit (see p. 19)*, to diminish another culture's originality, or to pretend to have full comprehension of a foreign topic by simply switching into one's own lingua. So even if a nation is not strong enough to impose its own language over another's, like Germany could never conquer the Chinese people, it could always try to steal important cultural property by giving it German names.

Language Imperialism	1
The End of Translation	16
The Revival of Confucianism (Interview)	24
Academia, Language, and Imperialism in China (Interview)	38
About the Author / Editors' Note / List of Chinese Terminologies	*66*

LANGUAGE IMPERIALISM

& The End of Translation

by
Thorsten Pattberg

lod
press
new
york

Printed in the United States

LANGUAGE IMPERIALISM

PART I

"The true victory (the 'negation of the negation') occurs when the enemy talks your language." --Slavoj Zizek

BEIJING - The *Frontiers of Philosophy in China* - a "distinguished" academic journal with an impressive editorial board composed of many prominent "China experts"- involuntarily supports Western sovereignty over the interpretation of Chinese thought. And it's not alone.

The Journal's open propaganda is striking: the word "philosophy" is a Western term and concept that is nowhere to be found in pre-colonial East-Asia. I would guess that 90% of China's population have never heard of "philosophy."

The Journal's title deliberately conceals from the public what China has instead. The correct Chinese term for philosophy, *zhexue*, is a late 19th-century import from Japan, where it is pronounced *tetsugaku*. It therefore cannot exist in any of the Chinese classics. Have a close look at the Journal's "Aims:"

> "Frontiers of <u>Philosophy</u> in China aims to disseminate new scholarly achievements in the field of broadly defined <u>philosophy</u>, and promote <u>philosophical</u> researches of the highest level by publishing peer-reviewed academic articles that facilitate intensive or extensive communication and cooperation between <u>philosophers</u> in China and abroad. It covers nearly all main branches of <u>philosophy</u>, with priorities given to original works on Chinese <u>philosophy</u> or in comparative studies in Chinese <u>philosophy</u> and other kinds of <u>philosophy</u> in the world." [highlighting by me]

Apart from the self-praise for being elite and exclusive (it tacitly offers the title "philosopher" to its authors) - and essentially an old-boy network - , the "Aims" section propagates the Western term "philosophy" no less than eight times (!). If this looks like ideological indoctrination, that's because *it is* ideological indoctrination.

We can only guess at how this propaganda pamphlet came into being; something along the lines of:

Junior editor: *"Hmm, that's awkward. We've chosen 'Philosophy' for our 'Title', yet we couldn't find the term 'philosophy' nowhere in the Chinese tradition."*

Editor-in-Chief: *"Don't be such a whiner. That's why we have to repeat 'philosophy' at least eight times in our 'Aims' section. It's Goebbels Law!"*

The Journal's mission is self-evident: to hammer home "Philosophy in China" in China and abroad. It is precisely this easy-peasy formula of parading Chinese thought under European prescription that should set serious scholarship on its ears. In its form it resembles fascist and ideological writings intended to forcefully pull a world-view, in this case the (Western) "History of philosophy,: over China's own contributions: prominent teachings such as rujiao, daojiao, and fojiao, but also hundreds of very distinct xue (disciplines) and jia (schools).

Most Western sinologists spent the formative years of their lives learning and mastering European culture and languages, an education that is guided by a colonial and imperial sense of mission. They inevitably continue old habits and cultivate a "China image" that is going to confirm their own world-view and advance the complete Westernization of China. They prefer to do it by translating China's socio-cultural originality into Western biblical or philosophical taxonomy. If nothing else, it's grand intellectual property theft.

Western publishers understandably embrace such ideology. How else can we explain - given that no "philosophy" existed in China - thousands of recent book titles such as *Readings in Classical Chinese Philosophy* (2006), *Introduction to Classical Chinese Philosophy* (2011), *A Short History of Chinese Philosophy* (1997), *Oriental Philosophy* (1979), and so on?

There are exceptions to this propaganda, of course, as seen in neutral titles like *Chinese thought* (1960). Yet, even that author had to work in the word "philosophy" somehow onto his book's front cover for promotional purposes, because that's precisely what the West wants: the foreigner without the foreignness. In fact, in all major Western schools, universities, news-agencies, and publishing houses there prevails an unparalleled hostility against foreign words.

I will go so far as saying that there isn't a single living English or American writer, editor, journalist, or professor who hasn't yet internalized the *6 Rules for Writing*, or derivatives of thereof, by no other than George Orwell, the father of dystopian authoritarianism and author of *Nineteen Eighty-Four*. Rule No. 5: "Never use a foreign phrase, a scientific word, or a jargon word if you can think of an everyday English equivalent." And that's just the post-racial, so-called (Anglo-Saxon) free world; using Chinese (or worse: Arabic, Turkish, or Hindi) words in German writings is violently unthinkable, even in this 21st Century. What a relief to hear that skin color is no longer an issue in free America and tolerant Europe, as long as those immigrants don't pollute our languages.

One can often guess from the book titles what ideology the publishers and the authors are trying to instigate. For example, Cambridge University Press - maybe because it served British imperialism for so long - is the usual offender; its title range includes propaganda like *Chinese Philosophy* and *Virtue Ethics and Consequentialism in Early Chinese Philosophy*, and so forth. On the other hand, Harvard University Press is explicitly more tactful in its title choices, for example in *The World of Thought in Ancient China* (1985) by Benjamin Schwartz.

Most Western universities and those that harbor Western-educated Chinese scholars require their students to write essays, class assignments, and to attend seminars on "Chinese philosophy" as if it was a fact of life that the Hellenic and the Judeo-Christian tradition also apply to the Chinese one.

Many upright China historians, such as Ji Xianlin, Tu Weiming, Gu Zhengkun and Roger T. Ames, persistently warn against misleading biblical and philosophical Western translations of non-Western concepts, but few people outside the profession have heard about their critique. Meanwhile, Western language imperialists pick cultural China into pieces... word by word.

In these days only those students who are receptive to Western indoctrination may reach a doctoral level, post-doctoral level, lectureship and then, finally, a professorship, by which time they will have become so soft and subservient, and will have "manufactured" so much propaganda material on "Chinese philosophy," that they cannot possibly blame anymore an omnipotent Big West for having deceived them or forced them to do so. Such a confession would stall their academic careers and immediately jeopardize their good reputations as reliable peer-reviewers and loyal cross-quotation careerists.

There are thousands of Chinese scholars who still fight for Chinese terminologies, but who will not be given a voice in Western mainstream media. Such Chinese are virtually unemployable globally, as they do not conform to Western *lingualism*. Indeed, how can any Chinese intellectual participate in a global conversation if Chinese words are categorically denied?

Often, Chinese scholars involuntarily support the Western onslaught on Chinese terminology and, without giving too much thought to it, they increase the Western hold for power over the history of thought. China's universities have come to a crossroad where they either sink into obscurity or define themselves but what they are not: Western outlets. Peking University's Department of Philosophy, The Council of Research in Values and Philosophy, in 2007 published its pamphlet "Chinese Philosophical Studies" entitled *Dialogues of Philosophies, Religions and Civilizations in the Era of Globalization*. All those key words in here: philosophy, religion, civilization, globalization are Western ones. Chinese concepts are knowingly left out of world history. And if Peking University, the superstar of Chinese higher education, encourages this voluntary cultural suicide, how much worse could it get?

PART II

"Avoid foreign languages […] It is a bad habit. Write in English." --William Strunk & Elwyn Brooks White

SHANGHAI - Many Western observers remain blissfully ignorant about the Chinese language and refuse to adopt Chinese terminologies into their China reports. They instead describe and interpret Chinese culture on the back of their own Western taxonomies and concepts. As if the West was the end of history.

You don't believe it? Read the recent *The New York Times* article "A Confucian Constitution for China" by "Confucian philosopher" Daniel A. Bell. It's about China but it doesn't include a single piece of Chinese terminology. As if the *Times* ordered Professor Bell to keep his China text Anglo-Saxon, clean, and unpolluted.

He is not alone. You may not be aware of this, but powerhouses like Germany prefers its China experts to be ethical German, and its China textbooks written in clean German diction, as if the Chinese people, their lexicon and their socio-cultural originality, did not serve any purpose at all in the history of humanity. The Germans call it *Chinabild* or "China-image," but it really is this: a China without Chinese.

The Germans wouldn't doubt for a moment the fact that the German language was essential to understanding their own culture. Yet, for foreign cultures it's exactly the opposite: as far as the German media and academia are concerned, foreign cultures precisely cannot be understood unless translated into familiar dictum.

And it gets worse. We know that the billions of East Asians in the world throughout history were thinking and giving names to their inventions all the time. Why is it that European countries, which barely hold 0.8-1.2% of the world's population each, are blending out all of that Oriental originality?

What is wrong, for example, with Europe adapting Chinese concepts like *ru*, *wenming*, and *junzi*; or Hindu concepts like *dharma*, *karma*, and *prajna*? Why do Europeans fearfully gatekeep their cultures from an inflow of Eastern originality?

Some commentators have argued with me, that the West is *full*. Full as in "no more capacity to learn." It is true that exotic Chinese concepts like *kungfu*, *yin* and *yang*, *fengshui*, and *Tao* have already made Western historians who still suffer from self-importance due to a history of colonialism feel weary and insecure. How to "Westernize" so many Asians who still have, after a hundred years of Western indoctrination, so many non-Western ideas in their heads?

Meanwhile, Hindi concepts like atman, avatar, yoga, nirvana and pundit make the United States look less Christian by the day. But wasn't Christianity supposed to be superior to all? There are tens of thousands of Eastern concepts that are censored out of the Western system just to keep the illusion of a universal Judeo-Christian manifest destiny alive.

Germany is case in point, where the ruling class controls the general public to live in an artificial German world (except for English loan-words, which are forced upon the Germans for historical reasons), and demand all immigrants to express knowledge solely in the form of German language. By that, the German dictionary becomes a tool for national coercion and subjugation, idea theft and thought plagiarism. Although not written in its preamble, the dictionary effectively tells its users: "Use the words in this book to make any idea or thought *ours.*" There isn't a deutsche school in the world that does not teach its pupils how to shun foreign words. Knowledge in Germany exists only if it's known in German.

As a result, German scholars, submerged in clean German culture, are destined to misappropriate China's history, etymologies, experiences, ideas and originality and, most importantly, they will intuitively omit (and who is to punish them for it?) the correct Chinese names of decisively non-German concepts and hide them from the German public. German China scholarship behaves like an organized syndicate –protecting their language turf and fighting off foreign gangs.

Not a day passes in North American and European media without some politicians, feuilletonists, or journalists lecturing China on "democracy" and "human rights;" words that are, you may have considered this, Western vocabularies and therefore cannot exist in China.

Tourists and imperialists do not come to be taught. They call things the way they call things at home: Most Western academics, existentially dependent on their nation states (they are state-employees), frequently replace Chinese originality with Western biblical or philosophical translations, or choose Western words and simply annotate them with the shallow signifier *Chinese-*, and thus present exactly the image of China they want to see: a place of zero originality.

There are now "Chinese religions," "Chinese saints," "Chinese gods," and "Chinese universities" all over the place. Yet, you will find that what these scholars translated from - the words *jiao*, *shengren*, *shen*, and *daxue* - do not bear any historical or cultural resemblances to those Western terms.

Confucius once said: "If the names are not correct, speech is not in accordance with the truth of things." What we see in Western 'China Studies' is a fraud. It's absurd to talk about "Chinese philosophers" when 90% of the Chinese population have never heard or read about such a word. They have *shengren* in China.

We may call late 20th-21st Western "China Studies" the greatest intellectual property theft of all time. In world history, it should rank besides another Western cruelty: the evils of the Christian missions to convert the common Chinaman.

We call our age the "Age of Knowledge"; yet ask the average American or European to name a single Chinese concept: the answer will be "none." They will talk about Chinese religion, Chinese food, Chinese culture ... they don't know a single correct word or taxonomy.

Human nature is not like this; nature has made people curious and inquisitive. The Western public would have loved to know what a *shengren* was, if only the media had printed this Chinese word, ever. I believe it is the nature of their nation states, their language policies and their self-serving education systems, that keep the Western public in the dark about foreign cultures.

Human knowledge is the combined originality and inventiveness of the human race expressed in all its traditions and languages.

But the truth is some people would rather see your language die.

THE END OF TRANSLATION

BEIJING - Few people realize that the Bible discourages people from studying foreign languages. The story of the tower of Babel informs us that there is one humanity (God's one), only that "our languages are confused." From a European historical perspective, that has always meant that, say, any German philosopher could know exactly what the Chinese people were thinking, only that he couldn't understand them. So instead of learning the foreign language, he demanded a translation.

Coincidentally, or maybe not quite so, History with a capital *H* followed the Bible. At the time of the Holy Roman Empire of German nation, when German scholars still spoke Latin, the German logician Christian Wolff got his hands on a Latin translation of the Confucian Classics. His reaction, I think, is as funny as it is disturbing: He reads *Kongzi* in Latin and says something like "Great, that looks very familiar, I have the feeling that I totally understand this Confucius!"

Wolff was so overjoyous with his new mental powers, that he went on to lecture about the Chinese as if he was the king of China. He is one of a kind; and very comical. Among his unforgettable findings were: "The Motives of the Chinese", or "The Final Purpose of the Chinese," and many more revelations.

And, of course, when somebody occasionally asked master Wolff why he didn't visit China, the greatest German sinologist of all time played out his greatest intellectual triumph. He replied that "the wisdom of the Chinese was generally not so highly valued that it was necessary to travel there for its sake."

It's thus pretty much established, I think, that history got an heart attack with this Wolff, or at least became too tired and too cynical. He sufficiently demonstrated that just about any European could become a China expert without knowing a single Chinese term.

Since this was true for just about any foreign language; so now we know why the German philosopher Immanuel Kant could reasonably announce the "End of All Things," and Georg

Hegel could proclaim the "End of History." Both learned men knew very well that they hadn't mastered any non-European language in their life-time; and they simply assumed that all History was like that too: lazy and European.

This attitude in the Western hemisphere has not changed, with the effect that we live in a crazy world today. Most American and European scholars believe that the Chinese "speak their languages", only that they "talk" in Chinese. Take the case of *democracy*. You may have considered this, but this is European word and concept and does not exist in China at all. Imagine China would return a favor and pressure Europe day-on day-out on becoming a better *wenming* or establishing a worthy *hexie shehui*.

Translation, of course, is an old human habit. That doesn't mean we shouldn't question it. It was our habit to slay our opponents in battle, but we don't do that anymore (except in just wars against the Middle East). Why do we still destroy foreign key vocabularies? Well, we first do so, I think, for psychological reasons. If Germany censors all important foreign terminologies, the German public is lead to think it alone knows everything there is to be known in the world, and - metaphorically speaking - behaves like it.

That's why Germany has produced so many world historians and philosophers, such as Gottfried Leibniz, Georg Hegel, Max Weber and Karl Marx. Academics call it *deutungshoheit* - meaning having the sovereignty over the definition of thought.

It might sound very depressing, but truth must be told: the West knows little about China, and cultural China has never become a truly global phenomenon. Not a single percent of the educated European citizenry, in my estimation, knows what *ruzang* is, or a *junzi* or *shengren*. And those are some of the most important Chinese concepts there ever existed for three thousand years.

To put it another way: have you ever wondered why there are now philosophers and saints all over the east, but that there has never been a single *shengren* or buddha in the west? Think about it, what is that probability? Whose version of history are we taught? The East has been preyed upon and is bleeding out of its socio-cultural originality as we speak.

I often feel embarrassed for some Asian professors (who got their "qualifications" in the West) when they open yet another department of "Chinese philosophy" or "Chinese religion" in China, often smiling into the faces of Western businessmen, missionaries and benefactors.

"Philosophy" is a Greco-Hellenic concept that is syndicated by the Judeo-Christian tradition. Rujiao, Fojiao, and Daojiao are all *jiao*, teachings. As to "religion" there is only one, the Western conception: We all live in the year 2014 of the Lord Jesus Christ. The so-called "freedom of religion" has to be understood as: "in this Christian world, you may believe whatever you want." China is already evangelized precisely because all "Chinese religions" adopted Judeo-Christian taxonomy to make their case and plea for inclusion in the Western curriculum.

China is not alone. India, too, is slowly figuring out there is something odd here. The Sanskrit-Hindu tradition invented tens of thousands of unique non-European concepts that are simply blocked out of History by Western media and scholarship. As if billions of Chinese and Indians in 3,000 years never invented anything - as if they just stood there waiting to be stripped of their intellectual property —their ideas, their names, their everything.

Some commentators have argued with me that we needed a global language, and today's English was the best candidate. To this I reply, are you crazy, that's exactly what the Germans once did; now it's the Anglo-Saxons who close their history book and announce: "We already know you."

No, the true global language would be radically different from today's English. It would need to adopt the originality and the tens of thousands of words provided by humankind's other language traditions on top of it. The end of translation, or should we say the liberation from misleading translations, would be a world revolution, and a revelation: it would remove boundaries and limitations and empower cultural originality and integrity. Under the motto of all words being created equal, the true global language would make us *all* freer, smarter, and better people.

Every language learner has this from time to time: a subconscious certainty that something is lost in translation, every time, without exception. Yet, most of us are too fearful to follow our gut-feeling through.

Maybe there is a hidden flaw in the story of the tower of Babel - a monstrous, frightening one. What if our languages are not confused at all, but any single group of human beings were just never enough in numbers to explore all the world's possibilities? What if the Chinese had invented things, and named them *tianxia*, *wu-wei*, *wu-xing*, *taiji*, *zongfa* and so on, that no American has ever thought about in this particular way, just as it always has been the case -I think we agree on this– with American ideas that China so keenly adopted?

It is often said that *language* is the key to understanding the Chinese culture and tradition. The question is which one should it be?

THE REVIVAL OF
CONFUCIANISM

Interview on *Shengren, Ruxue,* and the Rise of Chinese Terminologies

The following interview, conducted by Min Weiyuan of Tsinghua University, was precursory for preparing a show entitled 'Confucianism and the World' for Blue Ocean Network (BON TV). The show was cancelled in August 2012 due to the strains of the global financial crisis. This raw transcript is what remains of it:

MIN Weiyuan: *Shengren* as a concept is often misunderstood, even by Chinese people, especially by the younger generations. You've mentioned that this term cannot be translated into English. Why is this so?

Thorsten Pattberg: I believe that the *shengren* are a category of their won –like the buddhas in Buddhism. The word cannot be translated without becoming inexact and clumsy. There is a great misunderstanding in the West about China, largely because many Chinese key words are recklessly translated into European biblical and philosophical language. It is outrageous.

MW: Do you think it is taught in today's China: the concept of *shengren*?

TP: It is certainly taught into China because you can't separate Confucianism from the Chinese language. Just like Christianity informs European thought, so does Confucianism inform the Chinese one. Think about Confucian virtues such as *ren, yi, li, zhi, xin, zhong, xiao, jie, cheng, shu, lian, chi, liang, wen, gong, yong,* and *rang*. You can't separate them from China; those are genuine Chinese concepts. And they are remembered and honored with the Chinese written characters.

MW: How do you explain to laymen what a *shengren* is?

TP: The *Shengren* is an un-European concept. It is the highest member in the Chinese family tradition. A sage, a wise man who acts upon the highest virtues, called *de*. He practices self-cultivation and becomes something like a connector between all the members of the family, the nation, and, finally, the world and beyond.

MW: The strong appeal of Confucianism and the adherence to its traditional teachings are more obvious in Japan and South Korea than in China. True? There is growing appeal of Confucianism in Europe, especially in Germany. Why is it so? What is its appeal; and is the earlier assumption of a diminishing attachment to Confucianism in China true?

TP: To answer the last question first, again, you can't separate Confucianism from the Chinese language, that's one thing. Second, the Japanese culture that you've mentioned and the Korean culture by the way also share key concept originated from the Chinese civilization. The *shengren* in Japan is *seijin,* the same Chinese character (Kanji); and in Korea the word is spelled *seong-in.* So, there are shengren cultures all over East-Asia. You also have common (Asian) values here. The next one is, I think that the Confucian tradition has a great potential in the west, especially at the moment in Europe and Germany. Why am I saying this? Because at the moment Europe tries to unify; it tries to create a single European family. The Confucian way is the way of learning, the *daxue:* learning how to cultivate one's character. It is also about how to cultivate able leaders, leaders who are moral people or *haoren* (cultivated persons). Some become *junzi* (gentlemen). One day, who knows, we may even witness the first European *shengren.* Last, in political Europe we see the rise of a lofty Confucian pragmatism. That is something Europe aspires to.

MW: What is the strong appeal of Confucianism in Germany?

TP: The Germans are studying China very carefully at the moment, but there is still this murky confusion about the real Chinese tradition. Again, like I've said, most Chinese key terminologies are translated into German words from the Judeo-Christian tradition, sprinkled with Germanic folklore. The result is that China, at this stage of 'China Studies', is still totally *unknown* to the vast majority of the German public. That is another reason why Confucianism now has such a great appeal: It's a *new thing* in Europe.

MW: You mentioned in your articles that Western 'China Studies' is not up to its task, since all it does is attempting to *westernize* China's "social-cultural originality." How can the West learn to respect and adopt Chinese terms?

TP: It is very difficult at the moment because it seems to be the case that western terms and taxonomies dominate all Cultural Studies. I'll give you an example. I'm not happy with the definition of Confucianism labeled as "religion." Why? Because "religion" is a Western concept. There is really only *one* religion in the West and that is Christianity. We are living in the year 2012 which is the anniversary of the birth of our Lord Jesus Christ. Confucianism is not a "religion," in my understanding, but is *jiao* -a teaching. The correct name of that teaching is "ru" –the way of the literati. Thus, a *rujia* is a learned man; it can also be a *learned family* or *school* of that tradition. Social scientists in the west will yet have to pick up those correct Chinese names.

MW: What's the biggest weakness in China Studies?

TP: I wouldn't say it is weak. I would say it is criminal. Again, the language, I'm coming back to the problem of translation: If you don't adopt the Chinese concepts, you will never get a deep understanding of China. The English language is on the move to become the sole global lingua, and I'm happy with this. As you know, I'm German, but I *had to* learn English to be heard. We scholars have no choice. But I say why not picking up the key concepts of those various other civilizations we encounter and study? No harm in that. On the contrary, we will build a more complex, more authentic global humanity.

MW: We are seeing diminishing morals, lack of personal responsibility, and rising apathy in China. Why is it so? What factors led to this phenomena?

TP: I'm not sure whether this is just a Chinese thing. We are seeing a lack of morality all over the world, and I think it has to do with the ruthlessness of capitalism and this eternal competition for resources, but also with an overflow of information that creates helplessness and angst. People can look up their situation on the internet these days and what they find out is that life is deeply unjust, immoral, and unequal. Life is unfair, cruel, and most of us can't achieve what we wanted to. That includes the aspirations of governments. All those contradictions, the fast pace of our birth-run-die existence, the limited choices we are presented with… It's all one big downer. That's why people are constantly looking for new forms of spirituality. Confucianism is very appealing because it offers a code of conduct on how to become more successful in life, to cultivate a good work attitude, a love for learning, a sense for family and social order, and it offers almost 3000 years of culminated exegesis, commentary, and literature. It's time-proven.

MW: Could China's spirituality and morality go global?

TP: It's difficult to say. How can China globalize *anything* if it can't even defend its own key traditions from being destroyed and translated by Western media and scholarship? China is permanently seen as a place of zero originality. As to the decline of morality in

China, there's a certain negativity among Chinese intellectuals about their own global brand. Chinese society suffers from a lack of sympathy and empathy for the sufferings of its fellow citizens, especially if they don't belong to one's family or close circle of valuable connections (*guanxi*). We saw this in the case of little Yueyue, the little baby girl who was rolled over twice –by a car and then a truck– in broad daylight and on a busy street. The poor girl was left to die because apparently it was noone's business to help her. Does this tragedy speak for a nation? I think so, yes.

MW: Some in the West praised China for being more accommodating than ever before in terms of religion and religious beliefs. Others argue that China's fast development is nothing but a vacuum cleaner, sucking the spirituality and age old tradition out of its people. Do you agree?

TP: Everyone in the West since the French Revolution and the separation of Church and state aspires a more secular society based on scientific findings and reality. Faith, superstitions, and religious dogma should all be playing but a personal, subordinate part of life.

China already has achieved such secularity. Compared to fanatic America, "God's blessed country," China did a good job at keeping cults and religious extremists at bay. Other than, say, the United States and Germany, which are both run exclusively by Christian parties, China is lead by a secular government. That said, the starving wolves are still roaming in the woods.

MW: Different religions on the rise again in China?

TP: People are searching for identity and personal truth. There's so much to do in China. We are talking about Confucianism this time, but, of course, we also have Daoism and Buddhism, and pockets of Christianity, Islam, and Judaism in China. Such a variety of traditions should be appreciated, but, of course, there's always the danger of fundamentalism, especially in Confucianism which traditionally encouraged hierarchy, patriarchy and nepotism. The danger of a new Confucianism is that it may become *elitist*, that is to say a spiritual exercise reserved for a tiny elitist club.

MW: Can Confucianism survive and compete with other age-old traditions you mentioned?

TP: Oh yes, it can survive, there's no doubt about it. But it needs considerable investment. I don't think Confucianism is in physical competition with anyone at the moment because Confucianism is more like an attitude towards life than an organized movement. You can imagine a *Confucian* Jew or a *Confucian* Buddhist simply because Confucianism is a commitment to learning and scholarship, to family and to the state, so there's really no clash with the supernatural Gods of the world religions.

MW: Harmonization with strong roots in Confucianism is heavily promoted by the Chinese government as a way of maintaining stability and social harmony. How successful is this?

TP: Yes, concepts like *hexie shehui, datong,* and *tianren heyi* come to mind, all referring to ideas about harmoniousness and oneness. I think this is very successful policy. In Germany, our government promotes the concepts of solidarity and social contract. Those are principles that have guided our young nation ever since its founding in 1871. Such overarching social principles kit a nation together. China is twenty times as populous as Germany, has a vast, diverse territory, and was founded over two thousand years ago. Therefore, Chinese principles have a greater scope, depth, and background story to it. Before the rise of colonialism, the Germans had no concept of civilization –everything was just "culture" to them. But then they witnessed the British, the French, and the American empires, and they heard about non-European, fully-functional city states, and, all of a sudden, they were at a loss of words and thus had to adopt this new term "Zivilisation" into their dictionaries. Culture is the mind product of a people while Civilization is its physical manifestation. Think about architecture. That said, the Germans in this century will have to learn another new category, that of the Chinese *wenming*. A *wenming* is a above civilization and beyond culture –it is a spiritual realm created by and based on literati.

MW: As China becomes more capitalist, materialistic, individualistic and consumer based, how does modern China balance this new modernity with traditional harmony? Challenges? Future?

TP: Capitalism works fine with China. It is a success story. I honestly believe that China must not only compete for market shares, natural resources, and human capital, but also for its culture and terminologies. How come the West is flooded with goods produced in China, but not with words, ideas, and concepts produced in China? Others call this soft power. China, at this point in time, has no soft power whatsoever.

MW: With rapid urbanization, many citizens find themselves moving between cities and regions. Do you feel that the Chinese are now losing part of their identity and their roots?

TP: No, I don't think it's a loss of identity; on the contrary, they are gaining more of it. In the past, you were just a citizen of, say, Shanghai. But now, many Chinese professionals have lived long periods of time in Shanghai, Beijing,

Hong Kong, or maybe even in Seoul or Tokyo; then, perhaps, they moved to Boston, Berlin, or Paris. Whether it be national or international mobility, or a combination of it, people move back and forth and change the backdrop quickly. As a result, they will associate themselves with the spirits of those cities. Those identities will add up. People never lose them.

MW: Last question: "One country, Two systems" How about the crisis of identity for the people in Hong Kong, Macau, and Taiwan, or for other ethnic groups in general, as China gets more and more centralized and ruled from Beijing?

TP: I agree with my colleague from Tsinghua University, Daniel A. Bell, co-author of *The Spirit of Cities*, that people form stronger identities with cities (or regions) than they do with the state. That's because there are certain things a states can't do. For example, China doesn't grant me, a foreigner, the rights of citizenship. Nor should I take it since I am already a German citizen and can by law only hold one passport. In a nutshell, I cannot become Chinese. Yet, I can easily become a Beijinger, a Shanghaier, or a Hong Konger. People fall in love with cities all the time. Same for the Chinese abroad. How easy it is to become a New Yorker, a Berliner, a Londoner, and so on. So, instead of focusing on national identity, cosmopolitans should be more concerned about the place they (choose to) live in and the people around them. It's the identity of place that counts. Or, as the saying goes: Location, location, location!

MIN Weiyuan (闵蔚远) or 'Wendy Min' is a journalist and freelancer with focus on globalism and China from the University of Technology Sydney, Australia and L'Universite de Caen, France. She also studied at Tsinghua University, China.

ACADEMIA, LANGUAGE, AND IMPERIALISM IN CHINA

Interview on Academic Imperialism and the Future of Global Language

Eric Draitser, from stopimperialism.com, sits down with Thorsten Pattberg, from Peking University, to discuss the distinction between linguistic imperialism and language imperialism, the future of global language, and the world as seen from Beijing.

Eric Draitser: Welcome back to Stop-Imperialism.com the stop imperialism podcast. It is my pleasure and privilege to have Dr. Thorsten Pattberg on the program. Dr. Pattberg is a lecturer and author based in China. He is the author of *The East-West Dichotomy*, *Shengren*, and *Inside Peking University*, three invaluable books that everyone needs to definitely check out. So, Dr. Pattberg, thank you so much for coming to Stop Imperialism.

Thorsten Pattberg: Eric, glad to be on your show. Thanks!

ED: I wanted to begin with a recent article that you published on *Global Research*. It was entitled 'The Frontiers of Academic Imperialism'. In the article you touch on a number of important ideas, so why don't we start with the central issue and that is if you could give your definition of 'Academic Imperialism' – what does that mean?

TP: What I am specializing on is China so I am mainly talking about Chinese things. What I observed during my long stay in China, especially at Peking University, is this: Western scholarship on China censors Chinese concepts. Those concepts are consequently left out of world history. And because this is an ongoing process it won't stop tomorrow, we must address this problem, ok: In China, only those students who are receptive to Western indoctrination may reach a doctoral level, post-doctoral level, lectureship, and maybe become professors even; but by which time they will have become so indoctrinated and subservient to Western conceptions about the world, that they will happily join in the destruction of their own culture.

ED: There is an interest point that you made, and in fact I wanted to get into it a little bit later in the interview, you know, about the hoops you have to jump through to get through academia and higher education here in the West specifically. But before we get to that I wanna go through one example that you touch upon in your article. You use the example of the word "philosophy" and the concept of philosophy as it is understood in the west. So, could you go into that example that you lay out in the article and then also about the term you used – ideological indoctrination?

TP: The word "philosophy" is a Western word. It is borne out of the Western tradition; we know that it is a Greek concept, and just by hearing this word the impression we Westerners get is that it includes all foreign while being firmly rooted in Western tradition; at the same time the word lacks all foreignness while we are solely referring to ourselves. So, as an example, a book entitled "The History of Philosophy" may include a chapter on Confucius [the Chinese thinker] or it may not; either way it would not fail to fulfill its title's promise. Philosophy wasn't even a word in China before 1871 when it was imported from Japan. In Japan a philosopher is called *tetsugakusha*. So before the European powers arrived in East-Asia, China didn't have a word for philosophy at all.

ED: Yes, and because of that it's almost incumbent on Westerners who try to explain Chinese culture in some sort of an academic way that they then have to put their imprint on it; it has to fit into the dominant discourse of Western narrative. It is really interesting to read some of the stuff that you've published on the subject because what I find is that even though I try, you know, to be this anti-imperialist to engage with all the other cultures, China especially is so foreign to me that it is almost difficult if not impossible to me to even understand the mindset.

TP: Yes, and that is probably because all those original Chinese, Japanese, and Korean terms are left out of history. We simply don't know about them. For example why would you call Chinese thinkers "philosophers?" They have their own archetypes of thinkers, one of them being *shengren*. And *shengren*, it is *seijin* in Japanese and *seong-in* in Korean, so as to patronize the East-Asians, are always translated as "Chinese philosophers," "Japanese philosophers," and "Korean philosophers." Metaphorically speaking we have already annihilated East-Asia's thought traditions and its archetypes. They are gone. We don't talk about them any longer.

ED: Right, in other words we are trying to transform them into our own Western understanding, a very important idea. And there is another, you know, you mentioned this ideological indoctrination, is that what you are referring to?

TP: I am not an expert on the philosophy of education, but, you know we have a standard curriculum in the West and in China about what we should teach. I grew up in the west and studied in Germany and Scotland, and I have never heard about anything Chinese during my time in Europe. I only heard about those Chinese concepts when I moved to the east. Western education now is lacking diversity and pluralism; it is deliberately blocking out a more Eastern educational view on things.

ED: That's a great point you make that even the exposure that we have to Chinese history and Chinese literature or any of the Asian cultures – it is always sort of framed in a Western understanding. I remember back when I was in a history class and in that class there was one section on China, Japan, and Korea and you would go through that in about two weeks and that was your quota of East-Asian history.

TP: Yes, excellent example. It is like that in many places. It is changing of course, but slowly.

ED: There is another topic of yours that I want to touch upon because it fascinates me, and that is the issue of language imperialism and linguistic imperialism. Before we even dig into those concepts – what do they mean, and I know that you always have been very careful to make a distinction between language imperialism and linguistic imperialism. Maybe you could flesh that out.

TP: Yes, very briefly, linguistic imperialism is the replacement of one language by another, more dominant language. It's a branch of cultural imperialism: one culture loses, and the other wins. Language imperialism, however, is like surgery. The language imperialist deliberately picks certain foreign concepts that he fancies to translate into his own lingua; and he does so in order to obtain what the Germans call '*Deutungshoheit*'. It means having the sovereignty over the definition of thought. So, because the imperialist talks in his own language he will feel much more comfortable when talking about his object of studies: foreigners. By categorically ignoring their foreign language, but never being wary of writing about their beliefs, habits, and customs, over time, the language imperialist is putting up pressure and is forcing those foreigners to respond to his remarks, using precisely those Western words and translations that were suggested to them. The result: it will never be a fair East-West dialogue but a Western monologue.

It is cruel, but that's language imperialism: targeting your opponent's single most important ideas and translate them into your own language. If he picks them up, he loses.

ED: You know, I have heard academics, scholars of many stripes, linguists and others who talked about these issues, but I have actually not heard anybody other than you making a distinction between linguistic imperialism and language imperialism, so why do you think this distinction is so important?

TP: Well, because linguistic imperialism is so general. We are all English speakers, but you know, I am not an English *native* speaker as you can hear. I had to study English in order to have a say at all. That must be true of many other people in the world right now, especially students who plan on studying the humanities. It is time to save what can be saved: We cannot convince a lot of people in the west to study the Chinese language, because it is logistically impossible. Besides, Chinese is complicated; it may take ten years to master it. But what we can do is we can pick the most important Chinese key concepts like *wenming, shengren, junzi,* *daxue, datong,* etc., and we adopt them into our writings. At least for me, that is my personal goal.

ED: Very good, and obviously a productive goal, I think. I heard you mentioned it and I think that was what you were referring to a minute ago with the German phrase that you gave, but I wanted you to clarify something that I wasn't clear on: the prerogative of final explanation – what exactly does that mean?

TP: It's called *Deutungshoheit.* I give a practical example: Imagine a German-Japanese conference, and that conference's goal was to define the role of the Japanese emperor. In Germany, emperors are called "Kaiser." So, of course, the German professors [attending that conference] are trying to talk about *Kaisers* – precisely: about *japanische Kaiser.* But now, the Japanese don't have Kaiser and they don't know the German history and ideas about emperors. Do they really want to go there and discuss with Germans experts Japanese history on German terms? I don't think so, and they don't need to do so, because the Japanese have no German *kaisers,* but they surely have a

Japanese *tenno*. Kaiser or Tenno, which one should it be? Since the conference is clearly about Japanese emperors, *tenno* ought to be the correct term. If the Japanese in this example don't get this, they will lose the *deutungshoheit* and fall victim to language imperialism.

ED: What I am thinking about this question and hearing you explaining it, it reminds me of the postmodern thinker Michele Foucault and the whole concept of power relations and it seems to me that this issue of linguist imperialism is really one of power relations.

TP: Oh yes it is, and Foucault is still good reading. Slavoj Zizek recently said, and I quote: "The true victory (the negation of the negation) occurs when your enemy speaks your language." Language imperialism is about power, you are right about that.

ED: Absolutely. I want a little bit switch to another article you wrote. I know I am jumping around a little bit but time is limited and there is so much content I wanna cover. You wrote an article entitled 'Language and Empire: My language, Your prison', and among the many interesting things that I found in there one very interesting quote was when you were referring to philosophers and the study of philosophy as, quote: "the world's greatest syndicate". Could you explain what you mean by that?

TP: I can't recall exactly what I wrote there. Let me think about it, yes, the philosophers originated as a school of thought in the Hellenic tradition, you know, Plato and his school of philosophy. They surely developed pretty fast and, actually, they got rid of what today we call the sages -the Greek *sophos*– another school of wise men and teachers. The school of philosophers got rid of its competitors, and by the time Christianity came along, the Christians took care of the philosophers and promoted them, so to speak. So today, it is what it is: a syndicate that has spread into all corners of the world. There is no need for a Chinese thinker to call himself a philosopher; it's a Hellenic idea! There is no need for a Chinese thinker because they have their own titles –*shengren, junzi, shiren, wenren, wenxuejia,* or *sixiangjia*. Why would they refer to themselves as philosophers? I mean, in the

West we are caught in this language prison defined by the syndicate, and we cannot even graduate from a university without getting branded as "Doctors of Philosophy" – PhDs, even if what we studied got nothing to do with it. We are prisoners of the philosophers' syndicate.

ED: Absolutely right, and another thing that occurs to me when you are saying that though is that there is another element to this syndicate, and that is really the money, the resources; in other words it is a syndicate in so far as they control and have the means and the power to fund academia through institutions and Wall Street and various other forms. They can control who is *in* and who is *out*. And if you espouse an ideology or an idea or a position that doesn't fit their narrative you are *out*. Therefore it is almost like an organized crime family or something like that along those lines.

TP: Well, I don't know if it's a criminal syndicate, I didn't want to imply that. But surely it is about conformity. Students today are trapped in a life of conformity.

ED: [laughs] I was also not suggesting that it was criminal but rather in understanding the methods of control. You know, for instance, I know many people who have been PhD students, who've gotten their PhDs and you know it's true to be a PhD you have to be a certain intellect, to have a certain ability, but the majority I have seen have simply mastered the art of school. And it is this being able to be a good student, to produce a good paper or to have a good work ethic – these are the things that get you to a PhD instead of say independent thinking or new ideas which often times are not in keeping with that dominant discourse.

TP: Yes, I absolutely agree. I mean, education should always be about producing new and exciting ideas for others, or about exploring new domains of knowledge, rather than just learning what is already known. There should be a certain type of freedom to challenge existing norms and conventions. And back to the language thing – of course there is some progress lately: If you think about the great cultures in the east, the Indians and the

Japanese and the Chinese, there are many of their original ideas, I call it their socio-cultural originalities, that are now streaming into our lifes. Think about words like *avatar* and *yoga* – these are Indian loanwords. And with Chinese it is the same, it is travelling. Most people in Europe will have heard about *fengshui* or *yin and yang*; and people who are into material arts probably know about *wushu, tai chi,* or *qi*. So there is progress. However, as a general rule, we only adopt foreign words from the realms of leisure and entertainment, not so much from the realms of politics, culture, economics, technology, and general writing. In fact, journalists, editors, and publishers, as well as most Western professionals, are encouraged to use clean and simple English, and to avoid foreign terms and jargon altogether. We just don't want foreign words polluting our writings.

ED: There is another point to be made and that is the relationship we've been talking about, you know, education or indoctrination or however you prefer to look on it and the actual nature of imperialism. So I am going to ask you a broad question and you can take this in every direction you like: In what ways do you think language imperialism and/or academic imperialism really serves to justify what we see all around us as Western imperialism and the imperialism of, say, the Anglo-Saxon or European establishment?

TP: Let me express it like this: It is always easy to assume the role of the victim. Many Chinese or Indian commentators [on Western Academic Imperialism] embrace this role with pleasure – the role of the victimized, and blame Western imperialism for it. But I would actually like to take this opportunity and empower them; to empower them in a way that they can use their own concepts, and thus will be able to challenge European or Anglo-American dominance. But this is a win-win situation for East and West in the end, I am sure of it. It is all about what we truly want: do we want a global humanity or do we just want a Western humanity?

ED: Very interesting point, and, you know, since my realm is to focus on geopolitics that makes me think that the developments that we have seen this year, for example the BRICS talking about the BRICS developing banks moving away from, say, a dollar-dominated world to a more multi-polar economic world. We see Syria in the headlines every day and Russia and China being on the opposite side of the United States. So we do see a growing trend of China especially but also Russia and others beginning to challenge Western hegemony at least in the political realm; so perhaps now we are seeing a trend in more broadly aspects than just politics?

TP: You mean scholarship is now trailblazing global trends? Yes, that might be indeed the case. After the BRICS economies and their political power caught up, global scholarship might focus on what those nations have to offer to the world *culture-wise*. As to this geopolitical game you hinted at, scholars should always be independent from politics and ideology. I am aware that the trend, though, goes into the opposite direction: scholarship aligns itself to powerful interest groups in order to obtain political favors, grants, sinecures, and all kinds of perks. Our so-called academic think–tanks or NGOs in China are often sponsored by Western parties or private benefactors who already have clearly utilitarian motives, for example spreading Christian ethics, democratic values, etc., to the developing world. It may be difficult for them to avoid the imperialistic path.

ED: One of the thing that we have seen in the last fifty years – at least in the West – has been a shift in academia from to some degree a reactionary type of mentality to what we call a "progressive liberal establishment." So how has this changed, if at all, the nature of academic imperialism?

TP: American imperialism is in full gear. Sorry, I said "American" but I meant Academic imperialism. Western academia is, of course, not exclusively Anglo-American, there are still some German, French, Spanish, and Italian pockets. Still, the Anglo-American *modus operandi* is unstoppable. Because of that, European scholars tolerate the Anglophone world informing all strata of European society and all academic disciplines; but they won't hold that candle to the Chinese, Russian, Indian, or Japanese folks. Europe is culturally open to the west, and closed to the east. That Anglo-Americans enjoy, expand, and exploit their language dominance, there is absolutely no doubt about. We know that, because the German Empire in the 19th and early 20th centuries had experienced a similar blast of confidence. Already the most famous German philosophers such as Leibniz, Kant, Fichte, and Hegel actively promoted German dominance over other languages and cultures, and defined rules how to keep that status quo. Leibniz famously encouraged his fellow Germans to use only "teutsche" [German] words to express ideas, because this is the *only* sure-fire way to expand the empire. Foreign loanwords absolutely had to be shunned. What good could come of littering the national language with alien words that hurt the eye and offend the ear. Of course, the German Empire was torn into pieces and is no more. But that old 'language trick', bold and time-proven, stuck around, was picked up by the resourceful Anglo-American archenemy, and is now used [against the Germans] with a vengeance.

ED: You know, one of the reasons why I was so excited to have you on the program is because there are very few people that I came in contact with that I think really have a good window into the mentality – the perspective or the mindset – of the Chinese and Chinese culture and I think a lot of that comes with the understanding of their language and the study of their culture which I have done only to a minimum degree. In any case, the famous work that some people may have come across from Chinese literal history is the *Romance of the Three Kingdoms*. And, of course, I read it in translation, but in translation are those famous opening lines: "Empires wax and wane, States cleave asunder and coalesce…" That, apart from being a beautiful line, is what people remember because of the nature of empire and what that says about history. So I'm wondering how does the historical understanding of empire show itself in the Chinese mindset today?

TP: Empire is a very European concept. An empire is a war-machine. It never stops, constantly expands and conquers, until it implodes. Not a single empire in human history survived. The Chinese translation of empire is *diguo*, meaning god country. Imperialism is *diguo zhuyi* or god country doctrine. The Chinese have their own, more peaceful version of unity, *tianxia*, meaning "all under heaven." It is a far cry from the European fatalism of nation state and empire. Like the blue heaven, it simply *is*. There is no Judeo-Christian or Islamic God that commands the destruction of the infidels and the submission of nature. There exists a unique, non-European type of humanity in China. I would even call it a "new domain" in the study of humanities.

ED: It is difficult for Westerners and even for those of us who are really open-minded to these issues to grasp how Chinese view many of the issues around us. One about the things that I was recently talking about with one of our guests was the fact that the Chinese tend to be understated and to sit on the sideline to a large degree in political affairs, geopolitical and economic affairs, and I think this is also part of the historical tradition, so if you read Sun-Tze (The Art of War) or something like this, they are talking about allowing the opponents to destroy themselves is the strategies of the warriors and something like that. I am always fascinated with the Chinese cultural perspective on some of these issues.

TP: Yes, the Chinese are rather *passive*, maybe this is what you want to say. Historically speaking, they were very passive -we know that now. I remind again of the great German philosopher Georg Hegel who wrote about the philosophy of history and coined many phrases about the famous Chinese *passivity*, one of them goes along the lines of the Chinese being destined to be dominated [by the West]. Of course, this is a rather sick philosophy; yet it was and still is the prevailing notion in academia today. Chinese culture is regarded as archaic, backward, and uncreative. Xu Guangqi, a famous Chinese mathematician, scientist, and humanist who collaborated with the Jesuits in the 17th century, once famously quipped that Chinese theories were only as good as there was a Western equivalent that confirmed them. All other Chinese theories were deemed unscientific or unfounded. Ever since the scientific revolution in Europe, the Chinese have been playing catching up with Western theories and technologies, however, as Benjamin A. Elman, the US historian, explains in his book *On Their Own Terms*, the Chinese were able to persistently carve out their own path in the sciences and the humanities. In other words, they *still have* their own theories. Think about Chinese medicine, Chinese education, Chinese politics, and Chinese social science, just to name a few.

They [the Chinese] have their own ideas about *everything* European and American; they are keen on improving themselves, and they are willing to take in some of our ideas about democracy, human rights, and the rule of law. These are all new concepts that came to Asia from the West, and the Chinese *processed* them, modified them, according to their needs and requirements.

But what do *we* study from the Chinese? What do *we* make of their cultural achievements? The answer is: little and nothing. In fact, there is a certain kind of pessimism in China, a sort of hopelessness, if you like. "They don't seem to understand China" is the common expression I hear from Chinese scholars. It is disheartening.

ED: Absolutely, and one of the things that always strikes me too is the fact that when people talk about China and the rise of China it is almost always, even if it is unintentional or unconsciousness, in a *sinophobic* way, like "the Chinese are growing in power" or "the Chinese are culturally growing" etc., so therefore we need to grow *even faster* so that we can continue to be Number One – that's essentially the American mentality. But I would say that extends to Europe as well, so let us say the Western civilization.

TP: Civilization, as described above, is the physical manifestation of culture. Western culture has always been materialistic (and America is not an exception), with various interest groups competing with each other over resources, better theories, and useful technologies, summoning their supporters of influential city dwellers. Democracy was born. The Chinese wenming is different, it is about an artistic people, a people of thought, a people that mastered the arts… yet here again I have never seen this word, wenming, published anywhere in Western media like the *Wall Street*

Journal or the *New York Times*, they would never mention [the existence of] it.

ED: You know, it is so fascinating that you say that, correct me if I am wrong but the idea that "civilization" in the Western mindset is in association with physical growth and expansion to more complex systems incorporating technologies and things like this, whereas wenming, the Chinese idea really refers more to the cultivation of the mind and the spirit, and so civilization in that sense really refers to the development of the individual and the society.

TP: That is a very nice definition that you gave there. There are many more examples: Take for instance the Western concept of a "university." Again, it is a Greek concept so we stay in the realms of the Hellenic tradition. The modern idea of a university is to create experts, but that was not always so –in the beginnings we trained polymaths, learned men that were trained in mathematics, the sciences, the arts, philosophy, and theology. Johann Wolfgang von Goethe is a good example of a polymath. He was a poet, novelist, playwright, statesman, critic, botanist, philologist, psychologist, meteorologist, geologist, anatomist, and a philosopher of sciences.

The Chinese call their institutions of higher learning *daxue*. For example, Peking University is *Beijing Daxue*. The term translates as "higher learning," but it is not a direct translation or derivative from the Greek word *universitas*. Instead, it is borrowed from an ancient Confucian text, The *Daxue* or The Greater Learning. The *daxue* is an instruction manual on how to become a *junzi* –the perfect gentlemen. The Chinese *daxue* were and still are spiritual places where individuals cultivate the self. The highest degree in China is not a PhD or doctor of philosophy, but a *boshi* –meaning an erudite master.

ED: Nice. One of the things that come to mind is Deborah Brautigam's book *The Dragon's Gift* which some of you may have read about China's penetrating of Africa economically. I am not getting in all of that, but one anecdote that she told in the beginning of the book had to do with Chinese explorers who had gone to Africa – I don't even know when that was, perhaps the 14th century – but what they did was instead of bringing back say gold or jewels or diamonds or whatever, they brought back samples of animals, you know, giraffes and other indigenous animals of Africa that could not be found in China. And that story at least to me strikes a chord because again it gets to the Chinese concept of civilization or *wenming*, the idea that they want to know, that they want to grow intellectually. So what they gained from Africa and their explorations is not raw materials or wealth but rather knowledge.

TP: I never studied the early Chinese expedition to Africa in depth, and heard there's a lot of controversy. In general, the Chinese explorers were never as aggressive, it seems, as the European powers. China never controlled the globe like the British empire did, evidently. Now I want to come back to the book you mentioned about the *Dragon's Gift*. I wrote an article entitled 'Long Into the West's Dragon Business'. The word "dragon," etymologically speaking, is a Western concept. The Chinese dragon is very different; the creature is called *long*. The *long* is friendly, wise, and inherently good. It is one of the twelve animals of the

Chinese zodiac (calendar). It doesn't resemble the typical Western dragon, you know, pear-bodied, spying fire, destroying villages, that sort of fierce monster. In the West, dragons exists solely for the reason to be slain by heroes such as Siegfried, Beowulf, or Saint George.

ED: You are absolutely right, and if you were to follow US politics you will hear countless examples, Mitt Romney's anti-China tirades come to mind, abusing occidental mythology, namely that China is this red evil beast to be slain. The imagery of a plundering dragon also plays part, I think, in parading China as a "currency manipulator," "wage under cutter," or "violator of human rights." I recall one dragon caricature in a piece by *The Economist*, 'A dragon stirs', about China's mismanaged big banks; and another one, 'What China wants', about how America should respond to the China threat.

TP: We do have prejudices against dragons, and we have prejudices against China, and the first step to enlightenment is to *acknowledge* that we have those prejudices. Back to the philosophy of language, the German philosopher Ludwig Wittgenstein once said that the "Limits of my language are the limits of my world." As long as we engage China solely on our own terms, we don't learn a single new thing. The Chinese *long* is precious.

ED: Well said. It was a real pleasure.

TP: Thank you very much!

This interview took place on Dec 16th, 2012, and can be streamed and downloaded at Anti-Imperialism.com. This version has been slightly edited for length and clarity. (c) 2012-2014 Eric Draitser

ABOUT THE AUTHOR

Thorsten Pattberg (PhD) is a German writer, philologist, and cultural critic. He was born in Hamm, Germany, and studied Chinese, Sanskrit, Indian and Buddhism Studies at The University of Edinburgh, Fudan University, The University of Tokyo, and Harvard University. He graduated from the Institute of World Literature of Peking University, and is the author of *The East-West Dichotomy*, *Shengren*, *Inside Peking University*, and many articles on Chinese-Western relations.

EDITORS' NOTE

The contents of *Language Imperialism* –two articles and two related interviews- are in the public domain and archived at www.east-west-dichotomy.com. Versions of the articles have appeared in *Asia Times*, Hong Kong, and *Big Think*, New York. The publisher would like to thank the two distinguished interviewers, MIN Weiyuan and Eric Draitser, for their interest and support.

List of Chinese terminologies *(mentioned in this book)*:

圣人 shengren

君子 junzi

大学 daxue

学 xue

哲学 zhexue

文明 wenming

孔子 Kongzi

大同 datong

和谐社会 hexie shehui

天下 tianxia

道 dao (or Tao)

道教 daojiao

德 de

阴阳 yinyang

天人合一 tianrenheyi

儒 ru

儒学 ruxue

儒家 rujia

教 jiao

五行 wuxing

太极 taiji

宗法 zongfa

龙 long

关系 guanxi

无为 wuwei

博士 boshi

理 li

义 yi

好人 haoren

诗人 shiren

气 qi

神 shen

文人 wenren

武术 wushu

仁 ren

风水 fengshui

文学家 wenxuejia

思想家 sixiangjia

C